SPINY
SEA STARS

by Christine Zuchora-Walske

Lerner Publications Company • Minneapolis

This book is available in two editions:
Library binding by Lerner Publications Company, a division of Lerner Publishing Group
Soft cover by First Avenue Editions, an imprint of Lerner Publishing Group
241 First Avenue North
Minneapolis, MN 55401

Website address: www.lernerbooks.com

Words in *italic type* are explained in a glossary on page 30.

Library of Congress Cataloging-in-Publication Data

Zuchora-Walske, Christine.
    Spiny Sea Stars / by Christine Zuchora-Walske.
        p.   cm. — (Pull ahead books)
    Includes index.
    Summary: Simple text and photographs introduce
the physical characteristics, behavior, and habitat of
the sea star.
    ISBN 0-8225-3765-6 (lib. bdg. : alk. paper)
    ISBN 0-8225-3770-2 (pbk. : alk. paper)
    1. Starfishes—Juvenile literature. [1. Starfishes.]
I. Title. II. Series.
QL384.A8 Z83   2001
592.9'3—dc21   00-009239

Manufactured in the United States of America
1 2 3 4 5 6 – JR – 06 05 04 03 02 01

Look!
What do you see in this picture?

It is colorful and bumpy. Is it a rock?

Surprise! This is an animal
called a sea star.

Many sea stars live at the
edge of the sea.

Other sea
stars live at
the bottom
of the sea.

Sea stars are different colors and sizes.

Most sea stars are no bigger than a dinner plate.

Sea stars are slow animals.

How do these slow animals
stay alive?

Sea stars are spiny!
Spines are hard bumps or prickles.

Spines poke out from the skin
of sea stars.

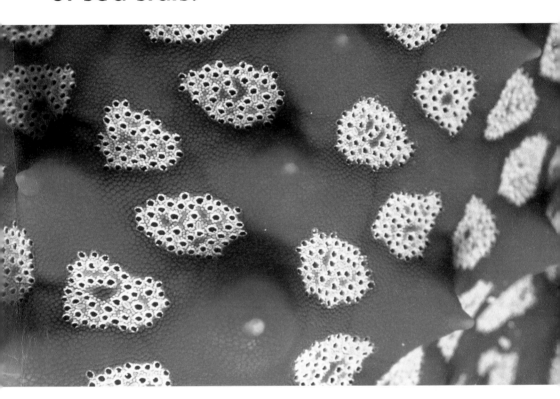

How do spines help a sea star
stay alive?

Most *predators* will not eat animals that have spines. Ouch!

Predators are animals that hunt and eat other animals.

Do any
predators
eat sea
stars?

A few predators eat sea stars.
This seagull is eating a sea star.

Every sea star has at least five arms.
Point to the arms on these sea stars.

How many arms does
this sea star have?

Some sea stars have
more than 20 arms!

If a sea star hurts its arm,
it can *regenerate* a new arm.

That means it can grow a new arm.

This sea star is regenerating
four arms.

Which arms are the new ones?

The arms of a sea star join
at the *central disk.*

The central disk is the round,
middle part of a sea star's body.

Under each arm are many tiny
tube feet. They look like straws.

Tube feet help a sea star grab things
and let go of them.

A sea star uses its arms and
tube feet to crawl.

How does this sea star see where it is going?

Sea stars have eyes, but they can see only light and darkness.

A sea star has one eye spot
on the end of each arm.

A sea star uses its eye spots
to help it find food.

The mouth of a sea star is underneath the central disk.

Sea stars eat small, slow animals.

Sometimes they eat dead animals,
like this dead fish.

This sea star is eating a mussel.
It pulls the mussel's shell open.

The sea star pushes its stomach into
the shell and eats the soft mussel.

Is this sea star eating?

No! It is squirting eggs into the water.
Sea star babies come from eggs.

Each egg grows into a *larva*.
A larva is a baby sea star.

A larva looks different
from a grown-up sea star.

A larva grows into a small,
young sea star.

These young sea stars look
more like grown-up sea stars.

Soon this sea star will become
a big, spiny sea star!

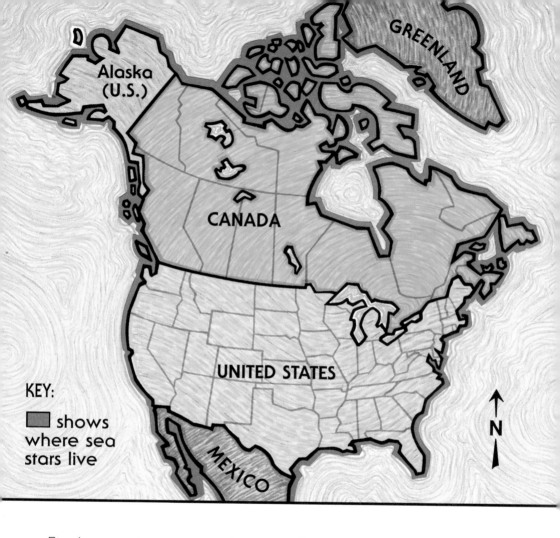

KEY:

■ shows where sea stars live

N

Find your state or province on this map.
Do sea stars live near you?

Parts of a Sea Star's Body

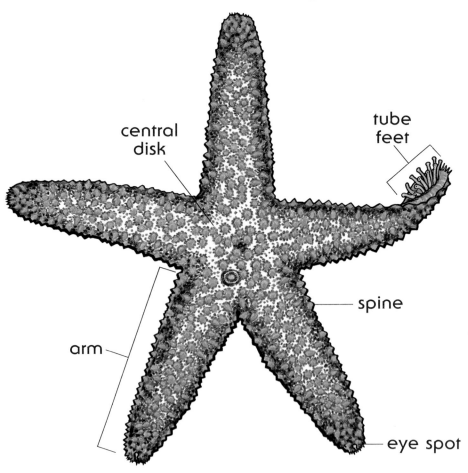

central
disk

tube
feet

arm

spine

eye spot

Glossary

central disk: the round, middle part of the body of a sea star

larva: a very young baby sea star

predators: animals that hunt and eat other animals

regenerate: to replace a hurt or missing body part by growing a new one

spines: hard bumps or prickles on an animal's body

tube feet: rows of suckers under the arms of sea stars that help sea stars grab and let go of things

Hunt and Find

- sea stars **eating** on pages 21–23
- a **predator** of sea stars on page 11
- sea stars **regenerating arms** on pages 14–15
- sea stars **squirting eggs** on page 24
- **tube feet** of sea stars on pages 17–18
- **young sea stars** on pages 25–27

The publisher wishes to extend special thanks to our **series consultant,** Sharyn Fenwick. An elementary science-math specialist, Mrs. Fenwick was the recipient of the National Science Teachers Association 1991 Distinguished Teaching Award. In 1992, representing the state of Minnesota at the elementary level, she received the Presidential Award for Excellence in Math and Science Teaching.

Ron Zuchora-Walske

About the Author

Christine Zuchora-Walske grew up in Minnesota. Later, she lived near Chicago for several years. She often visited Chicago's John G. Shedd Aquarium, and there she fell in love with all kinds of water animals. Christine enjoys doing anything outdoors—especially swimming. She also likes to read, make music, and write and edit books for children. Christine wrote *Peeking Prairie Dogs, Giant Octopuses,* and *Leaping Grasshoppers* for Lerner's Pull Ahead series. She lives in Minneapolis with her husband, Ron.

Photo Acknowledgments

The photographs in this book are reproduced through the courtesy of: **Tom Stack & Associates:** (© Randy Morse) front cover, p. 4, (© Gary Milburn) p. 17, (Ed Robinson) p. 18, (© Thomas Kitchin) p. 23, (© Mike Severns) p. 31; **Peter Arnold, Inc.:** (© Fred Bavendam) back cover, p. 24, (© Aldo Brando) p. 9, (© Ed Reschke) p. 11, (© Kim Heacox) p. 12, (© Jeffrey L. Rotman) pp. 19, 22; **Visuals Unlimited:** (© Hal Beral) p. 3, (© Rick Poley) p. 5, (© Daniel W. Gotshall) pp. 13, 21, (© John Forsythe) p. 14, (© John D. Cunningham) p. 16, (© Stan Elems) p. 20; **Photo Researchers, Inc.:** (© F. Stuart Westmorland) pp. 6, 27, (© E. R. Degginger) p. 7, (© Andrew G. Wood) p. 8, (© Andrew J. Martinez) pp. 10, 15, (© D. P. Wilson/Science Source) p. 25, (© Neil G. McDaniel) p. 26.